A Teacher in the Classroom:

Assignments From God

Michael Darnell Hill
AKA Analogy

A Teacher in the Classroom: Assignments From God
Kingdom Builders Publications, LLC

All scripture quotations, unless otherwise indicated, are taken from the Holy Bible, King James Version (KJV), Public Domain.

Amplified Bible (AMP)
Berean Study Bible (BSB)
Christian Standard Bible (CSB)
English Standard Version (ESV)
English Revised Version (ERV)
Good News Translation (GNT)
International Standard Version (ISV)
Message Bible (MSG)
New American Standard Bible 1977 (NASB 1977)
New International Version (NIV)
New King James Version (NKJV)
New Living Translation (NLT)

ISBN: 978-0-578-91144-1
Library of Congress Control Number: 2021909298
Printed in the USA

Authored by
Michael Darnell Hill

Editor
Lakisha S. Forrester
Kingdom Builders Publications

Cover Design
LoMar Designs

PREFACE

A Teacher in the Classroom is about God teaching and counseling me on life lessons. He had me to keep a record or account, which I call assignments, of every encounter that I have come up against and overcome during my spiritual journey. I've had many trials and tribulations, but God pulled me through all of them with His guidance. May this book serve as a spiritual guide and instructional manual as you go through your own spiritual journey.

CONTENTS

MH

DON'T BE TOO QUICK

SCRIPTURE

Listen for God's voice in everything you do, everywhere you go; he's the one who will keep you on track.

Proverbs 3:6 (MSG)

I had a dream the other day that the world was being flooded. I heard a still small voice telling me, "Jump in!" I replied, "I can't swim to save my life." The voice added, "I got you." So without hesitation, I held my breath and jumped in. The voice then said, "You don't have to hold your breath under here." I trusted that voice and began to breathe normally. As I began to lift my head out of the water to see what was going on around me, the voice said, "Wait! Put your head back under because there is a big wave of water coming." Just as it was announced, water passed over my head.
If I didn't listen to His voice or obey His

commandment, that surge of water that was headed towards me would've swept me away and wiped out the course God had set me upon. In my walk with God, I had to learn how to listen and wait patiently for Him to instruct me to move. He feeds me with His words so that I can gain knowledge and wisdom. And I became born again because He delivered me from my sins.

YOU ARE NOT GROWN!

SCRIPTURE

Like newborn babies, crave pure spiritual milk, so that by it you may grow up in your salvation.
1 Peter 2:2 (NIV)

I heard a voice echoing through my spirit saying, "You are not GROWN!" Hearing that bold statement made me ask the question, "What do you mean by I'm not grown?" The voice replied, "No, I'm not referring to GROWN as a physical aspect, but as a spiritual nature." The voice then added, "You have not yet developed spiritually and you're still spiritually immature. To confirm what I am saying, I'm going to reference you to **Hebrews 5:12-14**."

After reading that passage of scripture, I realized in that stage of my journey, I was still on baby's milk, the basics that we need in life in order to grow from infanthood to adulthood in Christ, when I should've been digesting solid foods long ago. The Lord has brought me a long way since then, yet I will continue to grow daily in Him. Amen.

SPIRITUAL PUBERTY

SCRIPTURE

When I was a child, I talked like a child, I thought like a child, I reasoned like a child. When I became a man, I put the ways of childhood behind me.
1 Corinthians 13:11 (NIV)

Spiritual puberty is the transition from our childish ways to maturity in the spirit. When we mature, our parietal cortex, the area of the brain that's associated with our self-awareness, awareness of others, and attention processing, is vital in our Christian life.

Spiritual changes of the mind as well as the heart affect each person differently. We cannot pinpoint an exact time when we will begin spiritual puberty. Our age doesn't measure our spiritual maturity. However, a spiritual experience can stimulate the brain to send signals to the heart to release control to the Holy

Spirit. Once control is released, we'll begin noticing changes in our minds and hearts that weren't there before. At some point in our lives, our minds start to gain knowledge and wisdom, and our hearts begin to feel love, compassion, and forgiveness towards ourselves and others. Our desire for God becomes stronger, and our love for Him becomes intense.

GROWTH SPIRIT

SCRIPTURE

If you declare with your mouth, "Jesus is Lord," and believe in your heart that God raised him from the dead, you will be saved. For it is with your heart that you believe and are justified, and it is with your mouth that you profess your faith and are saved.
Romans 10:9-10 (NIV)

To grow up spiritually over the course of our lives is the process known as a growth spirit. It's the development of our own feelings of inner power and strength that lead us to happier lives and taking full responsibility for our own actions.

We must have a willingness to accept what God is trying to feed us. He is not going to pour His words onto a silver spoon and force-feed us anything against our will. The choice is up to each of us to allow Him to lead. For us to grow spiritually, we must confess, accept, and acknowledge that Jesus Christ is our Lord and Savior. We must put Him first in all that we do.

SIGNS OF GROWTH SPIRIT

SCRIPTURE

Blessed are those who hunger and thirst for righteousness, for they shall be satisfied.
Matthew 5:6 (ESV)

God's words are never bitter, dry, or without flavor. **Psalm 119:103** states, "How sweet are your words to my taste, sweeter than honey to my mouth!" (**NIV**). Can you taste that sweet honey nectar dripping from His words?

The more we hunger for God's Word, the more we begin to grow spiritually. We cannot afford to fall asleep hungry. Not feeding on the Word before closing our eyes stunts our spiritual growth and causes spiritual malnourishment. When we hunger and thirst for God, our appetite increases. Once we begin to feed off God's Word, our spirit will keep coming back for seconds and thirds and so forth until it's satisfied. We will also begin to see an increase in the amount of biblical knowledge stored up in our minds and hearts, and notice all the different spiritual developments in our lives.

The Word of God cleanses out all the junk of unrighteousness, not just in our minds, but in our hearts as well. Day and night, we have to meditate on His Word until it becomes part of us. This promotes spiritual growth and helps us stay spiritually healthy and fit by providing us with the proper nourishments for our spirit. Our spiritual strength increases as we become stronger in the Word, which is where our righteousness comes from.

GROWTH RULER

SCRIPTURE

But do not measure the court outside the temple; leave that out, for it is given over to the nations, and they will trample the holy city for forty-two months.
Revelation 11:2 (ESV)

When trials and tribulations grab a hold of us and slam our backs up against the wall, in that moment, we may begin to question God's measurements on our lives. We'll likely ask Him, "Why are we going through this? Why is this happening? Why does that person have more than me?" We'll probably even stand back-to-back with an individual and measure the length of our success to theirs. If their success is taller than ours, we may begin to feel like we should be more advanced in life than them. However, we can't measure the length of our success to others. Some successes come from God, while other successes come from trampling over others to succeed. Discerning the difference is key.

God does not mismeasure; his measurements are precise. He measures us from the crowns of our heads to the soles of our feet. What He has for us is fitted and tailor-made just for us. Once we rule out how others see us and start measuring up to God's purpose for us, then we will begin to see the signs of our growth spirit.

GROWTH CHART

SCRIPTURE

And though your beginning was small, your latter days will be very great.
Job 8:7 (ESV)

Have you ever looked back on a time in your life when you felt small in the world? Can you see how God has brought you a mighty long way from where you were then to where you are now? I sure can. We may not be where we would like to be, but we are where God wants us to be.

For God to capture our struggles, pains, and disappointments over the years, He uses a spiritual growth chart. He marks the times in our lives when we had our backs up against the wall. God does not find a way for us. He makes a way for us by ruling out our past sins and mistakes so that we can begin to measure up to our purpose. He does not ignore or undo the past. He'll grant us peace with it so we can have a better future. He then uses a spiritual ruler to measure how much we have grown over the years.

Having strong faith in God promotes our spiritual growth, which is measured through God's grace. His grace is immeasurable because His grace is sufficient. It is God's grace that we are saved through faith. His grace allows us to see and feel that He loves, forgives, and saves us. It is with His grace that we hunger for knowledge so we can continue to grow spiritually. Therefore, we must continue to "grow in grace and knowledge of our Lord and Savior Jesus Christ" (**2 Peter 3:18, NKJV**).

So, if ever we begin to develop amnesia towards God's grace, He'll rejuvenate our memories by taking us back to the beginning to when we may have felt small, and then fast forward us to our glorious latter days.

READJUST YOUR FOCUS

SCRIPTURE

Because he has focused his love on me, I will deliver him. I will protect him because he knows my name. When he calls out to me, I will answer him. I will be with him in his distress. I will deliver him, and I will honor him.

Psalm 91:14-15 (ISV)

We may not all have 20/20 vision with our naked eyes when it comes to our ability to see what's in front or around us; hence causing us to trip, catching our feet on something that causes us to stumble or even fall. If we look through our spiritual eyes, we should see clearly what God has placed in front of us. God wants to have a relationship with us, and we should want to have one with Him as well. But how can we have a relationship with anyone, not just God, if we can't see eye to eye with that individual? How can we expect God to protect us or deliver us if we continue to walk blindly? Our focus must be adjusted to His view so that we can see what He sees for us. If our vision is blurred or impaired, we often stumble over our own blessings that God has placed in front of us.

FOCAL POINT

SCRIPTURE

Thy word is a lamp unto my feet, and a light unto my path.
Psalm 119:105 (KJV)

God wants to be the focal point. You see, He is the light that prevails, meaning He has superior power or influence in our lives. Once I became adaptive to His level of light, He then allowed me to see clearly. For so many years, I made a spectacle out of myself by not seeing that light to my path. I made some wrong adjustments. In order to bring my course into view, I had to adjust my focus. I had to align my focus on the centerpiece of everything that I believe in, which is God. Once I made those necessary adjustments in my life, everything else started to come into view. My purpose and goal, I could now see clearly. I often take a step back and just marvel at how God is working in and on my life.

A WORK OF ART

SCRIPTURE

So God created man in his own image, in the image of God he created him; male and female he created them.
Genesis 1:27 (ESV)

The Bible doesn't say we were created perfectly or without flaws. No one is, except Jesus. Since we are all created in the image of God and as representation of who He is, we were also created to be different from one another. Try to imagine how it would feel if God treated us according to our many flaws. I know it would not be a pleasant feeling. That's why He doesn't. So what would cause us to look and view one another differently? Why do we tend to give our own interpretation and judgment of others just by their differences? Why would we critique them based on their shape, color, flaws, and religion without even seeing them for who they truly are? What we see as differences, God sees as His beautiful, abstract artwork.

We as Christians are on display every day, being watched, observed, and judged by others. Being created in the image of God gives us the ability to see people not as they appear, but as God sees them. Since we are His creation, we must represent Him daily by placing His glory on display.

The Bible says that we are the light of the world (**Matthew 5:14**). Therefore, as the light, we cannot allow His glory to be displayed in the darkness, out of view from others. God's light must shine before others so they can see and be a witness to the glory of His beautiful artwork and creation. And just like an artist whose artwork is put on display for everyone to see, that is the same way that we should display our Heavenly Artist and Creator's glory. **First Corinthians 10:31** states, "Whatever you do, do all to the glory of God" (**ESV**).

HUMAN VESSELS

SCRIPTURE

Then he said, Go, borrow thee vessels abroad of all thy neighbors, even empty vessels; borrow not a few.
2 Kings 4:3 (KJV)

Vessels are floating containers used to carry and transport valuable cargo. Although they come in different shapes and sizes, they were all designed for the same purpose.

God created us as human vessels to contain the fullness of His Spirit and to transport His valuable cargo. He uses different types of human vessels—small, plain, and even broken ones. Broken vessels are those who feel like they are destroyed, forgotten, hopeless, worthless, and left floating out in the sea.

God would have us to dock our vessels at someone else's port. Then he would use us to transport or offload His valuable cargo, which is the gift of Jesus and all the possessions of love, righteousness, compassion, and forgiveness, into another human vessel so they could also contain and possess the fullness of His Spirit. We must be a willing participant to be used and anchored by Him, for whatever purpose He chooses for us.

He wants us to reflect His image. So He puts us through the process of refining fire, where He exposes our struggles and weaknesses. Even if we experience brokenness, He can still use us. All we have to do is cry out to our Lord and He will heal us. He'll gather up all our broken pieces and put them back together again. He'll bring our fears afloat so we can build trust in Him. Then He'll begin to mold and shape us into what He has created us to be and become.

SELF-CENTERED

SCRIPTURE

Let us make man in our image, after our likeness.
Genesis 1:26 (KJV)

Look at yourself in the mirror and ask your reflection what image it sees. Does it see an image of someone who perceives themselves as self-righteous, self-worthy, or valued? Or does it see someone who perceives themselves as being selfish, unworthy, or unvalued?

Our image is centered around our self-image, how we perceive ourselves—our ability, appearance, and personality. We were created to reflect God spiritually through our self-image. Sometimes for us to see our own image, the way God sees us, we may have to wipe away the condensation of low self-esteem, negative thoughts, and opinions from the mirror. I pray we all can see His clear reflection in us.

What's important in God's sight is our inner appearance and character. God does not want us to be overly concerned with our physical attributes because we could become self-absorbed with ourselves and how others perceive us, which puts us in critical lighting.

Critical lighting is when someone shines the light on one's imperfections, criticize their appearance, possessions, accomplishments, and tells them how they are not living up to their expectations, which can cause them to absorb and reflect that incoming negative energy and light. This will then leave room for one's inner critic to take center stage, entertaining those thoughts, and thus applauding criticism by agreeing to what their inner critic says about them. We are to cast off those defeated thoughts, because the Bible tells us that we are "fearfully and wonderfully made" (**Psalm 139:14, KJV**).

PRIDE

SCRIPTURE

Pride brings a person low, but the lowly in spirit gain honor.
Proverbs 29:23 (NIV)

Before Apostle Paul's conversion, he had an issue with pride. He thought too highly of himself and not enough of God. After conversion, he warned us all not to think of ourselves more highly than we ought to (**Romans 12:3**). Paul was given an imperfection, which was a thorn in his flesh (**2 Corinthians 12:7**). This imperfection helped him become the person that he should be through Jesus's strength rather than his own.

God uses our imperfections to remind us that we are not perfect. We must learn to embrace our imperfections because God does; they are necessary for growth. With an imperfect life, we should still give Him the glory that He deserves.

COULD YOU SPARE SOME CHANGE?

SCRIPTURE

Whoever is generous to the poor lends to the LORD,
and he will repay him for his deed.
Proverbs 19:17 (ESV)

Change starts in the heart. It is the catalyst that transforms the condition of our hearts from being bitter to being discerning, willing, and loving towards others.

There was once a beggar who stood on the same street corner outside of a coffee shop every day shaking his tin can vigorously asking for some change. Some people stopped and gave, but two individuals who went into the coffee shop daily saw this poor man, yet never stopped to even put any change into his cup. Instead, they walked right past him without even offering him a hello.

The beggar then changed up his approach to capture those individuals' attention. Rather than asking them for spare change, he asked them to spare time with him by having a cup a coffee, in which he offered to buy. One of the individuals stopped and took the beggar up on his offer because he realized he had forgotten his wallet at home. Instead of the beggar paying for the coffee like he offered, the waitress came up and said, "This one is on the house." Moments later, the individual found out the beggar had used his one free coffee a week on him. That day in the coffee shop changed that individual's heart. Now when he approaches the beggar standing on the corner, he offers to buy him a cup of coffee. He has learned to spare his time by giving to those in need.

God is intricately linked to the poor like a chain, therefore, giving to the poor connects us to Him. By giving generously, it also serves as an investment in our own lives, and God rewards us heavenly.

THE HITCH HIKER

SCRIPTURE

Do not neglect to show hospitality to strangers, for by so doing some people have entertained angels without knowing it.
Hebrews 13:2 (BSB)

There was a stranger standing on the side of the road with his thumb pointing towards the heavens looking for a ride. He was dressed in raggedy clothing and his beard was down to his chest. He had a red wagon with only three wheels that contained all of his possessions. Because of his outer appearance, some drove right past him, while others felt compelled in their spirits to stop and show him some hospitality.

Once the stranger entered the vehicles, he gave the drivers directions on where to go. While they were traveling down the byways and highways of life, he started telling them about Jesus and how wonderful and magnificent He is. At the end of their travels, the stranger handed the drivers a Bible and said, "Godspeed."

One driver then replied, "I have been down these roads hundreds of times in my life, but I was never shown this direction before." At that point, the driver realized that even though he was taking the stranger to his destination, he also found himself taking a different and better direction in his life. Sometimes Jesus will trust us enough to drive ourselves, but only if we listen to His directions.

GOD'S PLAN AND DESIGN FOR YOUR LIFE

SCRIPTURE

"For I know the plans that I have for you," declares the LORD, "plans to prosper you and not to harm you, plans to give you hope and a future."
Jeremiah 29:11 (NIV)

God has drawn up blueprints to help construct our lives. He spreads the plans out on the table in front of us, goes over them, then says, "These are the plans that I have for you and your future projects. And in these prosperous plans, I have outlined the steps on how to design it for you so you may have hope and a future."

Even when our plans are underway, it doesn't mean there won't be any delays in construction. Due to inclement weather, we all face delays or spiritual storms at some point or time in our lives. It is during these storms we must praise, pray, and trust God. Once the storm is over and the rain is gone, that's when we will begin to see our bright sunshine-filled days ahead. At that time, God will give His thumbs up to continue with our construction.

God takes us through different phases in our lives to get us where He wants us to be. The first phase in the construction of our future project is Laying the Foundation. **1 Corinthians 3:11** states, "For no one can lay any foundation other than the one already laid, which is Jesus Christ" (**NIV**). God starts by laying or pouring out His Word to form a solid foundation. It is His foundation on which we build our relationship with Him. We do it through praise, worship, and prayer. Without a strong foundation, we would not be able to withstand the spiritual storms that come our way.

The second phase is Rough Framing. **Psalm 103:14** states, "For He knows our frame; He remembers that we are dust" (**NKJV**). God formed us out of dust from the ground and then breathed life into our nostrils. When we first glance at our future, all we see is nothing but dust and dirt on the ground. But when God, the architect, comes in and surveys our land, He sees more for us than we see for ourselves. He then takes what He sees, begins to build it up from the ground level, and then breathes life into us. When God frames our future, He builds us a strong, solid infrastructure, one that holds us together during spiritual storms, and does not collapse once we step onto it. God fits all our good and bad experiences in life together, and then uses those experiences to shape or form our future. This infrastructure is a bridgeway that provides us with a cross over from the point we are now in our lives, over to the point where He wants us to be in the future.

Insulation is the third phase in the construction of our future. God uses the material from **Leviticus 19:17-18** to insulate the walls of our hearts. It reads, "You shall not hate your brother in your heart, but you shall reason frankly with your neighbor, lest you incur sin because of him. You shall not take vengeance or bear a grudge against the sons of your own people, but you shall love your neighbor as yourself: I am the Lord" (**ESV**).

God gives us the desires of our hearts if our hearts are insulated with His words. His words are used as a resistance barrier that blocks hatred, unforgiveness, and bitterness from seeping between the walls of our hearts. If this seepage reaches our hearts, it'll begin to erode and prevent the Holy Spirit from entering. Having our hearts professionally insulated by God's words reduces the amount of energy and time we spend or waste on hating others. God's insulation is used to protect the warm love inside our hearts from escaping, and the outside influences of the world from entering.

All that we do should line up with the Word of God. **Nehemiah 9:38** states, "In view of all this, we are making a binding agreement, putting it in writing, and our leaders, our Levites and our priests are affixing their seals to it" (**NIV**). Once we see that everything lines up with God's words, we then come into a binding agreement or covenant with Him by signing our name on the line, letting Him know we are ready to go forth with His plans for us. Once we commit to God's plans, He then stamps His seal of approval to start construction on our future project.

Remember, everything happens within God's timing. It may seem like a slow start to our construction at times, but God is teaching us to have faith, patience, and trust in Him. I can assure you that everything will be right on time. It's never over until God says it's over.

THE FINAL PHASE

SCRIPTURE

Whoever walks in integrity walks securely, but whoever takes crooked paths will be found out.
Proverbs 10:9 (NIV)

The final phase of our future project is the Walkthrough. This is when God walks us through every room or area in our lives where there have been cracks in our foundation and holes in our spirits, and shows us they have now been filled or spackled with the Holy Spirit. God takes us back to the point in our lives to where and who we were before, up to the point of where and who we are now.

In our final walkthrough, God gives us a detailed orientation on how everything should work and line up with His words. This is also when He informs us of our responsibilities and explains to us our warranty coverage, which is His protection plan for our now new project. God's Protection Plan coverage can be found in **Psalm 121**, verses **7-8**. They read, "The LORD will keep you from all harm—he will watch over your life; the LORD will watch over your coming and going both now and forevermore" (**NIV**). We must ensure that we always keep God's Protection Plan in a safe place in our hearts.

GOD'S SUPPORT SYSTEM

SCRIPTURE

I will say of the LORD, "He is my refuge and my fortress, My God, in whom I trust [with great confidence, and on whom I rely]!"
Psalm 91:2 (AMP)

There's a team building exercise called Trust Fall. It is when an individual falls backwards deliberately, trusting the spotter to catch them. For us to form a team building relationship with God, we must first trust Him. God is faithful and trustworthy. If we do fall, we have absolute faith and trust in His arms to be our spotter and catcher.

Temptations are the exact opposite—unfaithful and untrustworthy. If we were to fall backwards into 'their' arms, they will deliberately let us fall. But God provides us a way of escape from the arms of temptation (**1 Corinthians 10:13**). He's a true friend who stands before us all the days of our lives like no other friend, just like He did with Moses.

When we need someone to lean on, when we don't have enough strength to hold ourselves upright, God says, "Call on Me." He'll never leave us or forsake us (**Joshua 1:5**). He'll be that friend that we can rely on and trust in as our support system. He'll be there to prevent us from falling prey to the enemy. **First Thessalonians 5:24** states that, "God will make this happen, for he who calls you is faithful" (**NLT**).

LEARNING CURVES

SCRIPTURE

Those things, which ye have both learned, and received, and heard, and seen in me, do: and the God of peace shall be with you.
Philippians 5:9 (KJV)

You Can't Handle the Truth! In most cases, it's true that we can't handle the truth about ourselves, no matter which avenues they come from—family, friends, and even God. Learning those truths about ourselves could help to steer us straight in the right direction. If we allow ourselves to become distracted, we tend to lose focus and control when it comes to handling those truths.

Learning from our mistakes, having the courage to change them, and the willingness to accept the truth about ourselves is the learning curve process. While we're rounding the learning curves to our destination, we may collide or sometimes be blindsided by different issues—families, jobs, health, and finances—at different points in our lives. These issues could easily cause us to break down or even become stranded on the side of the road. When these issues happen, we should call on the services of Jesus, sit inside our vehicle, and wait patiently for Him to arrive with the tow truck to assist us. There is no need to step outside of our vehicle and look for someone else to help us. If we do, we'll then find ourselves standing outside of God's will, asking and looking for help with directions from some stranger passing by. Then we become upset at ourselves and wonder why no one is stopping to offer help or give us a ride. God says, "It's because they're not going the same direction as you."

The learning curves we face in life help us to improve our performance on the road to our destination. They increase change within us, growth in our lives and relationships, and help us to reflect on where and who we were at that precise point in our lives.

To me, there is no such thing as a smooth straight shot from point A to point B. Our destination is the point in our lives where God wants us to be. Before we can reach there, we must first go through Jesus to help guide us through those learning curves. Along the way, we will hit a few potholes, but we shouldn't let them discourage or reroute us.

When those potholes in the road begin to be filled up with the Holy Spirit, we may feel a little bump in the road where that emptiness and void were once there in our lives. God is letting us know that only He can fill that emptiness and void in our spirit. And for that purpose, we must put our hope in God and give Him all the praise and glory.

FINDING BALANCE WITH GOD

SCRIPTURE

A false balance is an abomination to the LORD, but a just weight is his delight. When pride comes, then comes disgrace, but with the humble is wisdom.
Proverbs 11:1-2 (ESV)

I remember going to the playground with my friend and getting on the teeter-totter (or see saw). I used to wait for him to jump on one end first and then I would jump on the other. When his end would go down, my end would automatically go up and vice versa. Since we both weighed the same amount, sometimes we would just sit there talking while keeping each other balanced on both ends. Once, when he jumped off abruptly without any warning, I quickly lost my balance and my butt went crashing into the sand. For a moment, I thought I had broken my tailbone, but I was fine.

We can't allow people to knock us off balance. We will never find that balance with Him, if we continue to keep our eyes focused on them. If our eyes are looking straightforward at God sitting across from us, He won't allow us to fall or get knocked down. Remember, we sit on one end, God is seated on the other.

God is that pivot point, the centerpiece, that we must come back to that helps keep us balanced. But if we teeter-totter in our lives, we may begin to lose our focus on God and not give Him the recognition that He deserves. The only way for us to stay balanced is that we must focus on Him. He's a trustworthy friend who would never forsake us by jumping off our teeter-totter hastily without any warning and leaving us with our face in the sand. He'll never look down on us, He'll look upon us, and give us a fair warning before any destruction.

TO BE MEEK

SCRIPTURE

Blessed are the meek, for they shall inherit the earth.
Matthew 5:5 (ESV)

Moses became one of the meekest and humblest men in the Bible. He recalled the last forty years of his life and saw that it was God's grace that made him the person he became. Yet often, people mistake meekness for a sign of weakness. Many have attempted to get a rise out of a meek individual, throwing hurtful words and lies at them, trying to knock them off balance with God.

A person of meekness has the power to control their anger. To do so, they must possess the power of humility and patience. **Proverbs 16:32** reminds us that, "He who is slow to anger is better than the mighty, And he who rules his spirit, than he who captures a city" (**NASB 1977**).

LIGHT WORK

SCRIPTURE

But those who do what is right come to the light so others can see that they are doing what God wants.
John 3:21 (NLT)

When we don the armor of righteous living, we take a knee and are knighted with doing what is right and by spreading the Good News about God. "So remove your dark deeds like dirty clothes, and put on the shining armor of right living" (**Romans 13:12, NLT**). It's time for us to step into the light.

Light is the source of goodness which avenges darkness. We have been hiding behind the darkness of our past and in the shadows of our fears for too long. We can no longer hide. "The night is almost gone; the day of salvation will soon be here" (**Romans 13:12, NLT**). God is light, and there is no darkness within Him. So take a quick peek and see that glimmer of light shining up ahead. Our spirit will speak to us and tell us it's safe to come out. Begin to walk slowly towards that light. The closer we get, the brighter the light will become. Once we step into that marvelous light, our eyes will readjust and gain focus.

There's a light switch inside of us that God must flip so that the light can shine through us and reflect on others. When we render to God, we are doing His will and not that of men. We must let our light shine before others, so when they see us coming towards them, they will first see the light reflecting from off our armor which bears witness to God's work.

When we do His work wholeheartedly, He then gives us a set of keys to His Kingdom. Once we open those Kingdom doors, we'll find salvation inside, which is only acquired by God's grace and our faith in Jesus. Then we will have access to bind whatever it is on earth and loosen it in heaven (**Matthew 18:18**). Hallelujah.

BURY THE HATCHET

SCRIPTURE

Bear with each other and forgive one another if any of you has a grievance against someone. Forgive as the Lord forgave you.
Colossians 3:13 (NIV)

When we say 'bury the hatchet,' are we truly doing that in our hearts and minds? When we truly forgive someone, we let it go. We take unforgiveness and hurl it so far into the depths of our past that our future won't be able to see it. If we were to leave the handle to our hatchet visible, readily accessible, out in the open, our hearts would see our carelessness. It would then retract, cause us to retrieve that hatchet at the very site, round up all the unforgiveness, and then use it to cut someone down. For us to settle any grievances that we might have with someone, we must bury the whole hatchet in a place that our hearts can't find.

HOARDING OF THE HEART

SCRIPTURE

Do not stay in the stronghold; depart, and go to the land of Judah.
1 Samuel 22:5 (NKJV)

An individual that hoards often has excessive amounts of items they find difficult in discarding or parting ways with. Their possessions are sometimes hidden or carefully guarded for future use.

Sometimes it's difficult for us to open the doors of our hearts and sweep out all the dirt and filth that have accumulated over time. We at times allow our hearts to hoard possessions, such as resentment, unforgiveness, hate, and envy, which makes it difficult for us to fully let go and love one another.

We then allow our tongue to manipulate our lips

to say that we love God wholeheartedly, but we haven't forgiven with our whole heart. Our hearts stronghold these possessions like a fortress, but love cannot reside in an unclean heart.

For us to part ways and throw out all unwanted junk, we must sort through our hearts carefully, boxing up and discarding certain possessions that we hide from family and friends in the back corners of our mind, a place where only we can go back to and find them later. For love to take residence in our hearts, we must clean out all those unwelcomed guests. For they are merely intruders invading the privacy of our hearts. The Holy Spirit is the landlord who evicts these unhealthy possessions so love can move in and have a place to call home. Our hearts provide a home for our love to live in. The Holy Spirit provides the roof that covers and protects our hearts.

The Holy Spirit is an activist that stands up against obstacles so we can have the free will to love. "Love is patient, love is kind" (**First Corinthians 13:4, NIV**). Love has so much more to offer. Love warms our hearts so that others don't have to be left out in the cold. Love is straightforward and tells us what we need to know and not what we want to know. Love is permissive and not possessive. Love has no fear. Love is an action, not an emotion. Love provides the foundation, in which being sincere, good, devoted, and honorable to one another is built upon.

THE BATTLE OF THE SPIRITUAL DETOX

SCRIPTURE

For God hath not called us unto uncleanness, but unto holiness.
1 Thessalonians 4:7 (KJV)

Physical detoxification is the process of removing impurities from the blood in the liver, where toxins are processed for elimination. In order for us to become more focused and more God oriented, we must go through a process of spiritual detoxification, where we give God authorization to enter into our homes and remove all impurities from within us so that our bodies can be cleansed from the inside out.

The enemy often calls and then disguises himself as a ram in the bush to throw us off balance and lure us away from our post, which is our temple. If we're not careful, we can think we're hearing

God's voice calling us from behind the rustling of that bush. When God calls, He'll supply us with all of our weaponry. When the enemy calls, he'll try to seize everything that God has supplied us with.

James 1:14 confirms that "every man is tempted, when he is drawn away of his own lust, and enticed" (**KJV**). Allowing our flesh to become tempted by the many diversions that we hear and see surrounding us, causes us to end up abandoning our post, leaving it unguarded and allowing the impurities to infiltrate our temple in attempt to overthrow and imprison our spirit.

Once these unclean spirits see that we have abandoned our post, they then dispatch their reinforcements, which are in the forms of our thoughts, words, and actions, to find a weakness or entrance into our temple. First, they think of strategic and deceitful ways to enter. Next, they'll begin to mix our thoughts together to form our words. Once our words are formed, they are then laid or poured out from our lips and cemented into a plan. After the plan is made concrete or hardened, they act by surrounding every wall and gate leading into our temple. Once they are in position and the signal is given to attack, the impurities will then use the desires of idolatry, greed, and lust as a ram to batter down our walls and gates. The objective of the impurities is to seek and contaminate anything that resembles joy, praise, holiness, and faith. Afterwards, they would then conduct a clean sweep of our spirit, not leaving one heart or soul unturned.

The Word of God is the only weapon of defense that can be used to annihilate and remove these impurities from out of us. To prevent them from invading us again, we must fast. By fasting, we seal off all entrances into our temple. As gatekeepers of our temple, we must reassure ourselves by praying in order to be able to distinguish between God's voice and the enemy's lies and disguises.

SURRENDER YOUR HEART

SCRIPTURE

Create in me a clean heart, O God, and renew a right spirit within me.
Psalm 51:10 (ESV)

When we surrender to God, we are submitting ourselves to His authority and completely giving up our own will in exchange for His will. We are giving Him the right and obligation to make decisions in our lives. God has placed a warrant out for each heart. But He's not going to chase us down or send out a search party to get it. He wants us to come and surrender it to Him voluntarily. But one thing is for sure, He will always meet us where we are.

Once we totally surrender our heart to God, He then takes and puts it into His protective custody or care. We also must hand all our paraphernalia of worrying and fears over to

Him. These anxieties must be confiscated by God and not put back into the possessions of our hearts.

Proverbs 4:23 says, "Guard your heart above all else, for it determines the course of your life" (**NLT**). For us to prevent corrupt speech escaping from our lips, focus escaping from our eyes, and our feet escaping from our paths, we must guard the perimeters of our hearts.

We must not allow our hearts to escape from God's protection and just be out in the world as a fugitive on the run, nor can we "copy the behavior and customs of the world" (**Romans 12:2, NLT**). That's like forging someone's signature that they did not authorize. But God can change any fraudulent heart into something new. When God is in our hearts, we do right, speak right, and live right. When He is absent in our hearts, we tend to do wrong, speak wrong, and live wrong.

FALL IN LINE

SCRIPTURE

Imitate God, therefore, in everything you do, because you are his dear children.
Ephesians 5:1 (NLT)

A leader is someone you can count on when needed. Someone who provides a solid foundation as a word of comfort. God was chosen unanimously to be our leader. As His children, we must fall in line behind Him. If we fail to follow our leader's actions and follow the actions of our emotions instead, then we are out of the game. **Proverbs 11:14** states, "Where no wise guidance is, the people falleth: but in the multitude of counsellors there is safety" (**ERV**).

At the beginning of our Christian walk, we don't know God all that well. But the more time we spend with Him, the more we know about Him. And the more we know about Him, the closer and deeper our relationship feels.

Many times, God places multiple faith believers in our way to offer advice so that we may receive godly wisdom in our life's decisions and choices. As Christians, it has been preached to us over and over to live by faith and not by sight (**2 Corinthians 5:7**). That's true. We should also be led by faith and not by emotions. God's Word and the advice of believers are confirmations that we use to guide our steps so we aren't led or lured by emotions. When we follow His leadership, we won't slip or fall down those steps; we'll be guided safely.

DO AS I SAY

SCRIPTURE

An intelligent heart acquires knowledge, and the ear of the wise seeks knowledge.
Proverbs 18:15 (ESV)

If we choose to select mixed emotions as our leader, that means we are being led or guided by them. If we allow ourselves to fall in line behind these emotions, we'll end up being lured into an emotional pit filled with bad decisions or choices.

We all know the story of the Garden of Eden in **Genesis, Chapters 2-3**, when God gave Adam and Eve instructions and guidelines on which trees to eat fruit from and not to eat from. He also gave them both warnings letting them know they would die if they disobeyed. So one day, while Eve was in the garden minding her business, the devil came up, disguised as a serpent, and spoke to her. He tried to convince her to eat from the forbidden tree by saying she would become like God. Eve knew what God had told them, but she allowed the serpent to lure and trap her into taking a bite of the fruit. Once the bait was bitten, Eve then lured Adam into doing the same. She took some over to him to eat. Once they ate it, they both felt ashamed for not following their leader's instructions.

Just like the serpent, our emotions come to us using different disguises, such as sadness, loneliness, anger, and fear, to convince us into going against God's instructions and guidelines.

LIGHTS, CAMERA, ACTION

SCRIPTURE

Therefore having girded up the loins of your mind, being sober-minded, set your hope fully upon the grace being brought to you in the revelation of Jesus Christ.
1 Peter 1:13 (BSB)

Emotions are not a stage play, so why do we continue acting on them? Wanting to look good in front of the cameras, emotions put on makeup to be noticed and alter people's perception about them. However, our actions stand front and center every day wearing no makeup while the world is watching. Our emotions attempt to direct or write the script to our lives, wanting all the upfront action. They try to upstage us into making wrong decisions so the camera would be focused on them. But we all know that God is working behind the lights and the cameras.

TOO MUCH INFO

SCRIPTURE

A good person produces good out of the good stored up in his heart. An evil person produces evil out of the evil stored up in his heart, for his mouth speaks from the overflow of the heart.
Luke 6:45 (CSB)

Playing good cop, bad cop sets the stage for our emotions. The good cop acts friendly, while the bad cop acts in an unfriendly manner to make you trust the good cop and tell them the information they want to know. Our emotions get us into an interrogation room, asking questions that sometimes they already know the answers to. Questions about our decisions and choices, hoping we'll confess and tell them something they can later use against us. **Proverbs 21:23** states, "Whoever keeps his mouth and his tongue keeps himself out of trouble" (**ESV**). Too much information opens the door to our lips, then comes ruin.

THE WITNESS

SCRIPTURE

But whoever denies me before men, I also will deny before my Father who is in heaven.
Matthew 10:33 (ESV)

Before the judge seats you, it is customary to take an oath by raising your right hand, while placing your left hand on the Bible. When we take an oath before God, we are vowing to give a truthful testimony. This was not the case in the Gospel of **Matthew**. In **Chapter 26**, Jesus told Peter before the rooster crows he would deny Him, not once, not twice, but three times (verse **34**), which came to fruition in verses **69-75**. When Peter was called to the stand to be a witness to the miracles that Jesus performed, he lied under oath, by not confirming the evidence he had observed with his very own eyes.

Just imagine you are sitting in a courtroom and

you hear your name being called by God to approach the stand as a witness to Jesus upon the earth. If we become surrounded by the wrong people, like Peter, we too can deny Him. This is evident if we speak untruthful or unkind words about others, conform to the world, have discourteous behavior, or borrow trouble and give it to others.

Remember, we are all made in God's image. As witnesses for Jesus on earth, our lives have to have a bright reflection on His image. If we deny Jesus, our lives would have a dark reflection on His image that no one could see. As Christians, we all should have personal testimonials based on evidence to what Jesus Christ has done in our lives to share with others, in hopes of leading them to Him.

FRIEND REQUEST

SCRIPTURE

And the scripture was fulfilled that says, "Abraham believed God, and it was credited to him as righteousness," and he was called God's friend.
James 2:23 (NIV)

The friendship of God and Abraham began in the 15th Chapter of Genesis. God told Abraham that he would have an heir to carry on his legacy long after he was dead and gone. Abraham laughed because it seemed impossible due to age (**Genesis 17**). However, God is always faithful. He is a promise keeper and a truth teller. If He said it, then it shall be done. Abraham was a hundred years old when Isaac, his promised seed, was born (**Genesis 21**). To test Abraham's faithfulness and loyalty, in **Genesis 22**, rather than using an animal as a burnt offering, God told him to offer Isaac as that sacrifice. Abraham trusted God and didn't hesitate. As he proceeded in his act of obedience, the angel of the Lord stopped him in the midst of his testing and supplied a ram instead. Because Abraham was unwilling to withhold his precious son from God, blessings exceeded him and his descendants forevermore.

Like Abraham, we too have the choice of accepting or rejecting God. Imagine you have a message from Facebook that someone is wanting to contact you. After viewing a limited profile, you see it is someone who is loyal, understanding, honest, and trustworthy towards His friends. Then you realize it is God sending you that Friend Request.

God is requesting that we be willing to spend quality time with Him. He wants us all to accept Him. He promises to always be there for us, but some choose to ignore or block Him from out of their lives so they can continue to advocate their worldly ways. But that doesn't stop Him from calling us unto Himself and continuing to send us Friend Requests. God goes back into the profiles of our hearts to look and see why we have rejected Him. When hearts are not compassionate, understanding, loving, warm, or affectionate, that is opposite of His desires for a relationship with us to be like. It's the impurity of the heart that rejects Him. Be mindful, if our hearts reject God, we cannot receive any of His messages until it opens.

So, if you're ready to Add God as a Friend and Father in your life, just press the Accept button in your heart to let Him in. The choice is yours.

BRAND NEW

SCRIPTURE

Therefore, if anyone is in Christ, he is a new creation; old things have passed away; behold, all things have become new.
2 Corinthians 5:17 (NKJV)

I dreamt that I owned a vehicle. It wasn't your ordinary type of vehicle. Mine needed work from the interior to the exterior. The engine was old, but it still started. The paint job reminded me of a bag of skittles because every door and the hood were a different color. Even though all these issues were going on, I still held on and trusted my vehicle to get me to my destinations, no matter how it looked. In that dream, my vehicle was fully restored.

Right now, I'm still in the restoration period by allowing God to restore me from the inside out. The more that I draw closer to and trust in Him, the more of the old me fades off, and the more like Him I become. Amen!

TEST DRIVE

SCRIPTURE

Little by little I will drive them out from before you, until you have increased, and you inherit the land.
Exodus 23:30 (NKJV)

Before we consider buying a new vehicle, we must first test drive it. To persuade us to buy their vehicle, the salesperson throws us a sales pitch. Before trust can be established, a personal relationship must be built between the salesperson and their potential customers. They must value the importance of their customers by being authentic, honest, and upfront with them. They may suggest a route for customers to travel to receive the full experience and feel of how the car handles the highway, gravel road, and sharp turns. They might even incorporate value added extras, such as workshops, car care clinics, and tutorials to solidify the relationships. Once a customer decides to buy the vehicle and drive it off the lot, its value depreciates.

Likewise, we are all God's potential customers. He throws us a sales pitch in attempt for us to want to buy into Him. God allows us to test drive His blessings so we can receive the experience and feel on how to handle them on the highways, gravel roads, and sharp turns in our lives. God keeps His promises, but we must build a personal relationship with Him first. He'll always be authentic, honest, and upfront with us. He values our importance. For our relationship to be solidified with God, He'll offer us His own value added extras, which are eternal life and entry into His Kingdom. But that's only if we follow the route in our lives that He suggests for us to travel. Once we decide to trust and buy into God and drive Him off the lot, our life doesn't depreciate; it elevates.

God wants us to experience the same promises He made to Moses and the children of Israel. **Exodus 16:4** states, "Look, I'm going to rain down food from heaven for you. Each day the people can go out and pick up as much food as they need for that day. I will test them in this to see whether or not they will follow my instructions" (**NLT**). God had a plan of deliverance for the children of Israel. They felt like His plan was taking too long and wasn't working out in a way they wanted it to, so they began to complain. They were already promised rich "land flowing with milk and honey" (**Deuteronomy 31:20, NKJV**), to live in homes that they did not build themselves, and harvest crops they did not plant (**Joshua 24:3**).

God didn't break His promises to Moses and the children of Israel, and He won't break them with us. God wants us to trust and turn to Him so that the rest of the people surrounding us would take notice and do the same.

HANDLING THE TRUTH ABOUT YOURSELF

SCRIPTURE

And ye shall know the truth, and the truth shall make you free.
John 8:32 (KJV)

Handling the truth about ourselves is like trying to steer a vehicle without any power steering. It's a struggle to do, but we still must attempt it. We shouldn't wear ourselves down or out by struggling with the truth when it gets harder to handle. The truth becomes easier to handle once we learn to accept it.

When tires on our vehicle become worn out and the threads begin to show, that's a sign that we need to change them immediately to prevent future problems up ahead. Our attitudes and hearts need changing immediately because they can wear us down or out and prevent us from reaching our destination. The threads in our hearts begin to be exposed to others when we choose not to accept the truth about ourselves. We can become angry with God and others for revealing those truths about us. When we get to that point, we have allowed our attitudes to deflate those truths. If we allow God to inflate the truth into us, then we can continue to move forward and closer to our destination.

SPIRITUAL ROADBLOCKS

SCRIPTURE

Trust in the LORD with all your heart and lean not on your own understanding.
Proverbs 3:5 (NIV)

As individuals, we often venture down different paths in our lives in search of our one true purpose here on earth. Every path we take is on our own account. However, it often seems like the path that's less traveled is the one we try to encounter the most. Sometimes we think we are on the right path until an unforeseen roadblock standing between us and what's on the other side is blocking our entryway to our purpose. A roadblock signifies for us to stop or go in another direction. God often puts these spiritual roadblocks in our path because we have failed to trust, listen, and be obedient to Him. These types of experiences often lead us to explore the bigger meaning of our lives, and what we discover is God's purpose for us.

REROUTING

SCRIPTURE

In all your ways acknowledge Him, And He shall direct your paths.
Proverbs 3:6 (NKJV)

Have you ever felt somewhere along that path in life you have drifted further away from your destination? Without a sense of direction, our purpose becomes adrift with no one to steer it in the direction of its destination. For us to hear God's voice telling us to reroute, we must turn on our God's Positioning System (GPS). God is reconfiguring and repositioning us back towards our destination because we have somehow veered off course, missed our turn, or began going down the wrong road. Many times, we ask God to take the wheel. But why do we tell Him where to take us? Is it because we don't trust Him, or is it that He'll take too long to reach our destination? If God took His hand off the wheel and allowed us to have control of it, we'll likely take too many shortcuts, and the only destination we will end up at is a dead end.

We don't know everything, and we can't figure everything out on our own. We can't assume that we know it all! We need to follow and listen to who is in front of us, which is God, and not what is behind us. Warning comes before destruction. By choosing to ignore the warning sign, 'NO U-TURN,' we find ourselves following and listening to our anger.

When we look into our rearview mirror at the enemy chasing us, at that very moment, we have taken our eyes off God and lost focus on our destination. The devil does not want us to reach the destination that God has routed us for. He tries to reconfigure it by causing us to miss our turn. But then God tells us to take the next turn coming up on our right.

God does not want us to worry or focus on what's behind us. He wants us to stay focused on what's ahead for us. In fact, in **Philippians 3:13**, the Apostle Paul said, "Brethren, I count not myself to have apprehended: but this one thing I do, forgetting those things which are behind, and reaching forth unto those things which are before" (**KJV**).

HIDDEN TREASURES

SCRIPTURE

For where your treasure is, there will your heart be also.
Matthew 6:21 (KJV)

God is the X that marks the spot in the center of our hearts, and we must endeavor to find those hidden treasures within. They are hidden from us, not because God hid them, but because we hid them from ourselves. The treasures of love, peace, forgiveness, and compassion are always present. Sometimes they are just buried beneath all that debris of pride. By pushing all that rubbish of pride to the side, we can then find the center, which is God, and discover what was in our hearts all alone. Without faith, we cannot detect where those hidden treasures are.

TREASURE HUNT

SCRIPTURE

You will seek me and find me when you seek me with all your heart.
Jeremiah 29:13 (NIV)

In our lifetime, we may become curious and embark on a treasure hunt or exploration in search of the where's, who's, what's, and why's, with no clues on where to begin. We ask ourselves these questions: Where am I headed? Who am I searching for? What will be revealed to me once I find it? Without clues, we tend to wander around lost in the darkness, running into our own thoughts of self-doubt. God doesn't try to hide Himself from us. He wants us to search for Him with all our hearts so that He can bring revelation to us.

God wouldn't send us on a scavenger hunt without first giving us clues on where to begin.

The first clue He gives us when we are in search for Him is a sense of peace. Peace pushes all that debris of confusion out of our minds, despite what's going on around us. The second clue that God gives us is confirmation. His confirmation lets us know we are headed in the right direction based on the choices we make. The last clue that God gives us is to follow His footsteps in the sand. When we follow them, they'll line up with His Word, which lets us know that we are on the right track in search of Him. Once we find and uncover what we're searching for, then and only then will God reveal Himself to us.

RELAY TRAINING

SCRIPTURE

Do you not know that in a race all the runners run, but only one gets the prize? Run in such a way as to get the prize. Everyone who competes in the games goes into strict training. They do it to get a crown that will not last, but we do it to get a crown that will last forever.
1 Corinthians 9:24-25 (NIV)

God puts us through a series of tests to prepare us for the future. He tests us on our faith, patience, and endurance. He wants to build up our character, hope, and strength so we can run in this spiritual race and not become weary or discouraged. Before we can compete, we must go into a strict training regimen, which comes through suffering, trials, tribulations, and unpleasant experiences in life. Our God would not just put us in the race untrained. We are not running solo. He is running alongside us so we can cross the finish line and receive the crown of eternal life.

STARTING LINE

SCRIPTURE

But if we hope for what we do not see, we wait for it with patience.
Romans 8:25 (ESV)

God has set us in the starting position for us to hear His voice and receive His messages. But we must be patient and wait for His instructions telling us, "On Your Mark, Get Set, Go!" If we take off sprinting before the sound of His voice is heard, we have just committed a false start, meaning we now have to return to our starting positions and repeat. Even though we can't see the finish line up ahead, our faith knows it's there. However, we still must wait patiently to reach it.

THE HANDOFF

SCRIPTURE

Then He said to them, "Take heed what you hear. With the same measure you use, it will be measured to you; and to you who hear, more will be given."
Mark 4:24 (NKJV)

For us to hear God clearly and take heed to what He is telling us, there must be a clean exchange of messages between Himself and us. This handoff must happen within the spiritual boundaries of our commitment, willingness to sacrifice, and total allegiance to Him. Anything outside of those boundaries disqualifies us from having a relationship with God.

God has the baton in His right hand, ready to place it in our left hand. But we must wait to receive His message before we begin sprinting. Otherwise, we can become too anxious and begin taking off prematurely, before we even receive the proper handoff from God. We can sometimes find ourselves looking over at our opponents and taking our eyes off God approaching us. If we lose focus on Him during an exchange, we would hear ping, ping, ping, which is the sound of the baton hitting the ground because of a botched exchange.

FINISH LINE

SCRIPTURE

I press on toward the goal for the prize of the upward call of God in Christ Jesus.
Philippians 3:14 (ESV)

There are other individuals running the same race as us. Just as God handed us the baton, He wants us to do the same to our teammates, even if we're familiar with them or not. They're still depending on us to hand them the baton successfully. We are all teammates in the eyes of God, striving to cross that finish line and enter His Kingdom.

SEEKING FULFILLMENT

SCRIPTURE

You, God, are my God, earnestly I seek you; I thirst for you, my whole being longs for you, in a dry and parched land where there is no water.
Psalm 63:1 (NIV)

There are two types of fulfillments: self-fulfillment and true fulfillment. Self-fulfillment basically states that one's personal achievements are more important than God's fulfillments. Once those needs are fulfilled, one then asks Him to leave until they feel He is needed again.

Many of us search for fulfillment in strange and unusual places, and try to use God as an escort. We'll call him up conveniently into our lives when we seek pleasure, and offer to pay Him with promises of drawing closer and seeking a relationship with Him. God cannot be found standing on a street corner waiting on us to pick

Him up.

True fulfillment only comes from accepting God into our lives, not for pleasure, but for true fulfillment. A relationship with God brings that fulfillment into our lives. He can only be found in our hearts when we continue to seek Him.

Genesis 5:24 and **Hebrews 11:5** speak of a man by the name of Enoch. Enoch was a man of great faith who walked with God. And because of his faith and walk with God, he was transferred to heaven without eyeing death. Before he was sent to heaven, he received a testimony that God was pleased and satisfied. Our faith and walk with God will also lead us to a righteous place of fulfillment.

DON'T SELL YOURSELF SHORT

SCRIPTURE

God paid a high price for you, so don't be enslaved by the world.
1 Corinthians 7:23 (NLT)

Do you sometimes feel unloved, unwanted, and undervalued? God knew we would experience these types of emotions in our lifetime. That's why **Ephesians 1:5** states, "God decided in advance to adopt us into his own family by bringing us to himself through Jesus Christ. This is what he wanted to do, and it gave him great pleasure" (**NLT**).

If we were to ask God how much does He love and value our worth, He would tell us to look in **John 3:16**, which states, "For God so loved the world that He gave his one and only Son, that whoever believes in him shall not perish but have eternal life" (**NIV**). Then He would say,

"Now that's how much I love and value your worth."

Even though He created us differently, we are all equal in God's eyes; that's why He calls us worthy. We should all know that we are valuable to God because we were bought at a high price through the sacrifice and the precious blood of His Son, Jesus Christ, on the cross. Yet, we often weigh our value on the scales of other people and the world's opinions of us. Our value shouldn't be measured on who we are, but on whose we are. God does not care about our titles, wealth, or social status. He cares about the condition our hearts are in. He cares about how we love and treat others. We as God's people should walk with true hearts of gold, which does not tarnish or corrode, and is worth more than any monetary value.

John 3:5 says, "Jesus answered, 'Very truly I tell you, no one can enter the kingdom of God unless they are born of water and the Spirit'" (**NIV**). God's Spirit gives birth and life to the spirit being inside of us. To be born of the spirit is new birth. That's why as believers we were chosen as God's children. New birth puts our heart in a right relationship with God. The more time we spend in His presence, the more we begin to bear the family likeness.

A TEACHER IN THE CLASSROOM

SCRIPTURE

I will instruct you and teach you in the way you should go; I will counsel you with my eye upon you.
Psalm 32:8 (ESV)

In a classroom, the teacher takes roll by calling out each student's name to see whether he or she is present or absent. It is the student's responsibility to be present in class, and thereby each is held accountable for his or her own attendance.

Holding grudges is like taking attendance in class. God calls out each grudge by its name, such as unforgiveness, anger, and bitterness, to see whether any are present. If they are indeed present, we will have to dismiss them from out of our hearts.

Ecclesiastes 7:9 states, "It is foolish to harbor a grudge" (**GNT**). The only way for grudges to be absent or removed is for us to forgive others, which will drop the grudges from our roll book and not allow them to take up a seat in our hearts. Grudges are like holding on to hot coals. We may think that by holding those fiery grudges we have against someone that we are burning them, but we are really burning ourselves. If we continue to hold on to them for too long, they'll leave a permanent mark or scar in our heart. To prevent ourselves from scarring, we must extinguish that fire from within and walk away from the flames.

We are more likely not to succeed in the school of life, but succumb to it, if we continue to have our grudges present. Instead, we should allow love, forgiveness, and warmth to fill up those vacant seats that were once filled with unforgiveness, anger, and bitterness.

NOTE-TAKING

SCRIPTURE

A disciple is not above his teacher, but everyone who is perfectly trained will be like his teacher.
Luke 6:40 (NKJV)

God is the instructor who teaches us on forgiveness, and like a great teacher, He also keeps His eyes on His students. He stands up at the chalkboard, with chalk in hand, waiting to write instructions on how we should forgive others and ourselves. As students, we are to take notes on everything He tells us to write, because He knows later in life there is going to be a pop quiz or test that we need to be ready for. God has an open book policy on test taking. For us to pass, we must refer to our previous notes we had written.

CHEMISTRY

SCRIPTURE

Spend your energy seeking the eternal life that the Son of Man can give you.
John 6:27 (NLT)

God examines our energy (interaction) with other forms of matter (people), as well as our hearts to see whether any unforgiveness is present. For us to have chemistry with God, we must interact with Him daily through prayer. Instead of wasting our time and energy on nonsense, we should use that same time and energy talking and listening to God. We'll receive His comfort and love by doing so. "For whoever would draw near to God must believe that he exists and that he rewards those who seek him" (**Hebrews 11:6, ESV**).

Our love towards God and unforgiveness towards others are like oil and vinegar. Both are attracted to their own kind; therefore, they do not mix because they are made up of different types of molecules. No matter how much you shake, stir, or even whisk them together, eventually they will separate. Our relationship with God should be like bonded molecules that don't separate, no matter how much we ourselves are shaken, stirred, or whisked.

The way we treat others can have a positive or negative correlation between God and us. Our heart is the correlation that measures the strength and direction of our relationship with God and others. Love and unforgiveness are made up of different types of molecules. Love is made up of actions, while unforgiveness is made up of emotions. Our love molecules are attracted to forgiveness and warmth, while our unforgiveness molecules are attracted to anger and bitterness. That's why these two different types of molecules can't be mixed in our heart. We say that we love God, but having unforgiveness, anger, or bitterness towards our brothers and sisters separate our spiritual bond with Him.

MATHEMATICS

SCRIPTURE

Do not add to what I command you and do not subtract from it, but keep the commands of the LORD your God that I give you.
Deuteronomy 4:2 (NIV)

God teaches us spiritual mathematics to help us solve the different equations in life in **Matthew 6:33**. It states, "But seek ye first the kingdom of God, and his righteousness; and all these things shall be added unto you" (**KJV**). So, the equation to our life's journey is GOD'S KINGDOM + HIS RIGHTEOUSNESS = ALL THINGS, which are not just considered material things. God wants to be the sum, that addition to our lives. He does not want to be subtracted or divided from it.

The equation of LOVE + FORGIVENESS – UNFORGIVENESS ÷ LOVE = GOD helps us solve the answers that we seek from Him. For our love to equal to God, we must subtract and cancel out all unforgiveness that divides us from love so we can truly find the sum of God. For love to be present in our hearts, we must add value (God) to the equation (relationships). Then we become wealthy by His instructions and teachings.

ABOUT THE AUTHOR

Michael Darnell Hill was born in Germany but raised in Bessemer, Alabama.

His spiritual journey has navigated him down rough roads in his life to get him to his destination. He considers his faith in God to be the centerpiece of his life, as well as the love and support of his family and friends who surround him in faith.

Michael writes under the inspiration of the Holy Spirit, and before his thoughts are penned down to paper, he prays and asks God to lead him what to write.

His goal in life is to touch as many lives as possible through his writings. He aspires to one day be blessed to write a stage play and movie.

www.ingramcontent.com/pod-product-compliance
Lightning Source LLC
Chambersburg PA
CBHW061126100726
47911CB00013B/703

* 9 7 8 0 5 7 8 9 1 1 4 4 1 *